THE FALL OF FREDDIE THE LEAF

A Story of Life for All Ages

LEO BUSCAGLIA, Ph.D.

Published by Charles B. Slack, Inc.

Distributed to the trade by Holt, Rinehart and Winston

Also by Leo Buscaglia

Living, Loving & Learning

Love

Because I Am Human

The Way of the Bull

The Disabled and Their Parents:
A Counseling Challenge

Personhood

Copyright © 1982 by Leo F. Buscaglia, Inc.

Library of Congress catalog number: 81-86645
Charles B. Slack, Inc. ISBN: 0-913590-89-4
Holt, Rinehart and Winston ISBN: 0-03-062424-X

Published in the United States of America by:

Charles B. Slack, Inc.
6900 Grove Road
Thorofare, New Jersey 08086

In the United States, distributed to the trade by:
Holt, Rinehart and Winston
383 Madison Avenue
New York, New York 10017

In Canada, distributed by:
Holt, Rinehart and Winston, Limited
55 Horner Avenue
Toronto, Ontario
M8Z 4X0 Canada

Printed in the United States of America
10 9 8 7 6 5 4 3

Charles B. Slack, Inc.   ISBN 0-913590-89-4
Holt, Rinehart and Winston ISBN 0-03-062424-X

Dedicated to all children who have ever suffered a permanent loss, and to the grownups who could not find a way to explain it.

This story is also dedicated to Ronald, Christina, Meredith, Stephanie and Julia, who are actively engaged in the spring of their lives.

And to Barbara Slack, my editor for the past 10 years, who will always be a most loved and valued leaf on my life's tree.

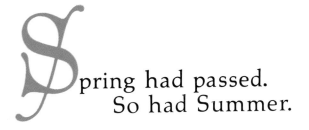

Spring had passed.
So had Summer.

Freddie, the leaf, had grown large. His mid-section was wide and strong, and his five extensions were firm and pointed.

He had first appeared in Spring as a small sprout on a rather large branch near the top of a tall tree.

Freddie was surrounded by hundreds of other leaves just like himself, or so it seemed. Soon he discovered that no two leaves were alike, even though they were on the same tree. Alfred was the leaf next to him. Ben was the leaf on his right side, and Clare was the lovely leaf overhead. They had all grown up together. They had learned to dance in the Spring breezes, bask lazily in the Summer sun and wash off in the cooling rains.

But it was Daniel who was Freddie's best friend. He was the largest leaf on the limb and seemed to have been there before anyone else. It appeared to Freddie that Daniel was also the wisest among them. It was Daniel who told them that they were part of a tree. It was Daniel who explained that they were growing in a public park. It was Daniel who told them that the tree had strong roots which were hidden in the ground below. He explained about the birds who came to sit on their branch and sing morning songs. He explained about the sun, the moon, the stars and the seasons.

Freddie loved being a leaf. He loved his branch, his light leafy friends, his place high in the sky, the wind that jostled him about, the sun rays that warmed him, the moon that covered him with soft, white shadows.

Summer had been especially nice. The long hot days felt good and the warm nights were peaceful and dreamy.

There were many people in the park that Summer. They often came and sat under Freddie's tree. Daniel told him that giving shade was part of his purpose.

"What's a purpose?" Freddie had asked.

"A reason for being," Daniel had answered. "To make things more pleasant for others is a reason for being. To make shade for old people who come to escape the heat of their homes is a reason for being. To provide a cool place for children to come and play. To fan with our leaves the picnickers who come to eat on checkered tablecloths. These are all reasons for being."

Freddie especially liked the old people. They sat so quietly on the cool grass and hardly ever moved. They talked in whispers of times past.

The children were fun, too, even though they sometimes tore holes in the bark of the tree or carved their names into it. Still, it was fun to watch them move so fast and to laugh so much.

But Freddie's Summer soon passed.

It vanished on an October night. He had never felt it so cold. All the leaves shivered with the cold. They were coated with a thin layer of white which quickly melted and left them dew drenched and sparkling in the morning sun.

Again, it was Daniel who explained that they had experienced their first frost, the sign that it was Fall and that Winter would come soon.

Almost at once, the whole tree, in fact, the whole park was transformed into a blaze of color. There was hardly a green leaf left. Alfred had turned a deep yellow. Ben had become a bright orange. Clare had become a blazing red, Daniel a deep purple and Freddie was red and gold and blue. How beautiful they all looked. Freddie and his friends had made their tree a rainbow.

"Why did we turn different colors," Freddie asked, "when we are on the same tree?"

"Each of us is different. We have had different experiences. We have faced the sun differently. We have cast shade differently. Why should we not have different colors?" Daniel said matter-of-factly. Daniel told Freddie that this wonderful season was called Fall.

One day a very strange thing happened. The same breezes that, in the past, had made them dance began to push and pull at their stems, almost as if they were angry. This caused some of the leaves to be torn from their branches and swept up in the wind, tossed about and dropped softly to the ground.

All the leaves became frightened.

"What's happening?" they asked each other in whispers.

"It's what happens in Fall," Daniel
told them. "It's the time for leaves
to change their home. Some
people call it *to die*."

"Will we all die?" Freddie asked.

"Yes," Daniel answered. "Everything dies. No matter how big or small, how weak or strong. We first do our job. We experience the sun and the moon, the wind and the rain. We learn to dance and to laugh. Then we die."

"I won't die!" said Freddie with determination. "Will you, Daniel?"

"Yes," answered Daniel, "when it's my time."

"When is that?" asked Freddie.

"No one knows for sure," Daniel responded.

Freddie noticed that the other leaves continued to fall. He thought, "It must be their time." He saw that some of the leaves lashed back at the wind before they fell, others simply let go and dropped quietly.

Soon the tree was almost bare.

"I'm afraid to die," Freddie told Daniel. "I don't know what's down there."

"We all fear what we don't know, Freddie. It's natural," Daniel reassured him. "Yet, you were not afraid when Spring became Summer. You were not afraid when Summer became Fall. They were natural changes. Why should you be afraid of the season of death?"

"Does the tree die, too?" Freddie asked.

Then, Freddie was alone, the only leaf left on his branch.

"Someday. But there is something stronger than the tree. It is Life. That lasts forever and we are all a part of Life."

"Where will we go when we die?"

"No one knows for sure. That's the great mystery!"

"Will we return in the Spring?"

"We may not, but Life will."

"Then what has been the reason for all of this?" Freddie continued to question. "Why were we here at all if we only have to fall and die?"

The first snow fell the following morning. It was soft, white, and gentle; but it was bitter cold. There was hardly any sun that day, and the day was very short. Freddie found himself losing his color, becoming brittle. It was constantly cold and the snow weighed heavily upon him.

At dawn the wind came that took Freddie from his branch. It didn't hurt at all. He felt himself float quietly, gently and softly downward.

As he fell, he saw the
whole tree for the first time. How
strong and firm it was! He was
sure that it would live for a long
time and he knew that he had
been a part of its life and it made
him proud.

Freddie landed on a clump of snow. It somehow felt soft and even warm. In this new position he was more comfortable than he had ever been. He closed his eyes and fell asleep. He did not know that Spring would follow Winter and that the snow would melt into water. He did not know that what appeared to be his useless dried self would join with the water and serve to make the tree stronger. Most of all, he did not know that there, asleep in the tree and the ground, were already plans for new leaves in the Spring.

The Beginning

It is difficult to capture the magic of nature but I feel that those responsible for the photography in this book have done just that. I would like to express my gratitude to photographers Anthony Frizano, Greg Ludwig, Ken Noack, Bobbie Probstein and Misty Todd-Slack. Together, we have all attempted to share the mystery of *Freddie The Leaf.*

Leo Buscaglia